Persuasion

Dark Psychology

How People are Influencing You to do What They Want Using Manipulation, NLP, and Subliminal Persuasion

By

James W. Williams

© Copyright 2018

All rights reserved.

The content contained within this book may not be reproduced, duplicated or transmitted without direct written permission from the author or the publisher.

Under no circumstances will any blame or legal responsibility be held against the publisher, or author, for any damages, reparation, or monetary loss due to the information contained within this book. Either directly or indirectly.

Legal Notice:

This book is copyright protected. This book is only for personal use. You cannot amend, distribute, sell, use, quote or paraphrase any part, or the content within this book, without the consent of the author or publisher.

Disclaimer Notice:

Please note the information contained within this document is for educational and entertainment purposes only. All effort has been executed to present accurate, up to date, and reliable, complete information. No warranties of any kind are declared or implied. Readers acknowledge that the author is not engaging in the rendering of legal, financial, medical or professional advice. The content within this book has been derived from various sources. Please consult a licensed professional before attempting any techniques outlined in this book.

By reading this document, the reader agrees that under no circumstances is the author responsible for any losses, direct or indirect, which are incurred as a result of the use of information contained within this document, including, but not limited to, — errors, omissions, or inaccuracies.

Table Of Contents

Introduction 8

Chapter 1 – Manipulation 11
   Where Manipulation is Found 12

Profile of a Manipulator 14
   Manipulation Motives 16
   What Happens to the Victim 18
   Profile of a Gas Lighter 20
   Subtle Manipulation 22

Manipulation Tactics 24
   Humor Aimed at Your Weaknesses 26
   Surprise and Little Time 28
   Lying About and Exaggerating Facts 30
   Giving You the Upper Hand 32

Manipulation as a Positive 33
   Positive Social Influence 35
   Not All Manipulators are Evil 37

Overcome Manipulation 38
   Know Your Worth 40
   Don't Be Afraid to Keep Your Distance 42
   It's Not Your Job to Change Them 43

Confronting the Manipulator 45

- Ask Questions 47
- Take Your Time 48
- Practice Saying No 50

Chapter 2 – NLP 52

How We Receive Information 54
- Your Personality Profile 56
- The Animalistic Nature of Our Brain 57

Our Map of Reality 59
- Meaning is Subjective 61
- We Can Change Our Feelings 64

How People Use This Against You 65
- Mimicking Body Language 67
- Cold Reading 69
- Confusing Phrasing 71
- Using Your Wants 73

Chapter 3 – Subliminal Persuasion 76

The Subconscious Mind 77
- Subliminal Advertising 79

Social Media 81
- Altering Perspectives 83

How You're Being Subliminally Persuaded .. 84
- Asking for More 85
- Doing Favors 86

Being Flattered	88
Tactically Choosing When to Ask	89

Conclusion 91

Thank you! 94

Your Free Gift

As a way of saying thanks for your purchase, I wanted to offer you a free bonus E-book called *"Bulletproof Confidence Checklist: Eliminate Limiting Beliefs, Overcome Shyness and Social Anxiety and Achieve Your Goals"*.

In this guide, you will discover:

- What is shyness & social anxiety and the psychology behind it
- Simple treatments for social anxiety
- Breakdown of the traits of a confident person
- Breakdown of the traits of a socially awkward person
- Easy, actionable tips for overcoming being socially awkward
- Confidence checklist to ensure you're on the right path of self-development

To grab your free bonus book just go to:

https://theartofmastery.com/confidence/

Introduction

It's never easy to feel like you might be getting taken advantage of. Whether it's a spouse, a friend, a relative, a child, a sibling, or even just the person that makes your coffee in the morning, anyone is capable of taking advantage of other people.

In the same way, anyone is at risk for being the person that is getting manipulated. Even the most powerful people might be under the influence of someone else's manipulation. Having control over another person is a very powerful feeling, and some people use this as their life source. Other people have been so controlled by others throughout their lives that they don't have an identity other than the one of their abuser.

This book aims to break apart three main ways that someone might be getting taken advantage of. There will be examples of how to identify this type of manipulation, and what can be done to stop and prevent further toxic behavior.

The first step in the recovery process is understanding manipulative behavior at its core. It's important to figure out what a manipulator looks like, and how they might specifically take advantage of other people. By understanding this you're better equipped to identify and defend against the manipulation.

This book isn't going to be about how to use these techniques on others to manipulate them. Manipulation is dangerous and it's crucial to understand the damage that this tool can do. Many people live unhappy lives because they have been so manipulated by others. It's time for that deception to end, and instead, you should be putting focus on improving relationships and overall self-esteem.

This book will also focus more on 1 on 1 persuasion, but it's still important to understand that there are certain medias that are taking advantage of you as well. Manipulation surrounds us, and it seems inescapable. While the manipulation won't ever fully stop, there are ways of preventing it from happening, and methods of attacking just how much it affects a person's life.

Just because someone is a victim of manipulation doesn't mean they might not also be a manipulator themselves. Often, the two go hand in hand. It's tricky behavior, but if more is known about it, there will be a better understanding of how to stop this toxic pattern.

Chapter 1 – Manipulation

Manipulation involves the emotional exploitation and distortion of one's mental processes in order to receive something that the manipulator wants. In certain abusive situations, it can sometimes be obvious that there is some form of harm being done. Manipulation is much trickier to identify, and many people will go a long time without realizing that they are being manipulated.

Everyone has likely manipulated someone else in their life. It's just a part of our average conversations and interactions. Sometimes, you might persuade someone to do something because you have an ulterior motive. Maybe you hear that your friend's going to be out of town for your birthday party, so you tell them how much fun it's going to be, hoping that they'll skip their trip. Though this isn't that harmful, it can be considered manipulation.

Manipulation starts in childhood. That can be

how many of us learn how to get what we want. Children are master manipulators, attempting to alter the truth, their feelings, and the emotions of their parents in order to get what they want. It's part of our childhood development. At some point, kids realize that they can't hurt people to get what they want, and as empathy develops, it's much easier to become less manipulative.

Manipulation can turn into a form of abuse when it is not properly monitored. There are people that grow well into adulthood, still manipulating the people around them. Some manipulators don't realize what they're doing while others might rely on this tactic to get what they want. Manipulation is very complex, and this chapter will unpack the basic understanding of manipulation.

Where Manipulation is Found

Manipulation occurs mostly within the closest relationships of another person. Spouses, parents and children, siblings, and relationships amongst best friends can become very manipulative. The people that surround us are the ones we look to when in need. We see our family and friends as those that provide us with something, at least to a certain extent. When some feel as though they might be in need of something that they can't easily get, they begin to manipulate a situation.

It can also be seen in the workplace often. Bosses might manipulate their employees in order to get what they need to reach a certain goal. Coworkers might manipulate one another in order to get ahead, often competing for positions that might change the overall fate of their lives.

Manipulation is also in the society around us. The way advertisers use our fears to make us buy certain things. The way political campaigners try to gain voters. These processes can become incredibly manipulative. The majority of this book will discuss one on one interactions, but it's important to be aware of how manipulative commercials, billboards, radio ads, and print media can be. There are many tactics that big companies use to get consumers to buy into certain ideas. This manipulation can be powerful, but when one becomes aware of the manipulation around them in their personal lives, they have an easier time of recognizing it in social settings as well.

Profile of a Manipulator

There are certain qualities that all manipulators have. Each and every person that has manipulated in their lives is different, however, the characteristics that make us manipulate are usually similar. There are certain reasons a person might become a manipulator. It might have been in their household, and the way that they were raised. Often, children of drug addicts end up becoming manipulators later in life, learning how to lie and deceive at an alarmingly early age.

A manipulator might have formed their habits later in life, covering up their own addiction or fear of failing. Manipulators might have learned that they can get what they want if they influence people in a certain way. Some individuals seem to have a certain charm to them while others couldn't lie to save their life. Manipulation is insidious, and the pattern of behavior can be incredibly hard to break.

This next section will go over what a manipulator looks like. Sometimes, you might have to do some looking inward. Not everyone wants to admit it, but there's a good chance that they might partake in some manipulation themselves. Even victims of abuse might manipulate, perhaps lying to friends and family about the level of violence they endure. Not all manipulators are bad, but the behavior itself is something that should be avoided.

Whoever a manipulator might be, they usually have a reason why they wish to take advantage of others. Those that manipulate aren't always aware, but they will have a certain goal that they are working towards.

Manipulation Motives

The biggest reason someone might be a manipulator is because they want to have a sense of control. They might have come from an unstable childhood, never finding a sense of self. They then struggle to identify themselves, feeling as though they don't have control over their lives. Some people will internalize this pain, becoming codependent on other people acting passively. Other people will be more active with their codependency, gaining a false sense that they can have control over their own lives if they can control others. They'll then manipulate a situation, attempting to have power over ones around them.

A manipulator will do whatever it takes to make someone else have a certain perception of them. As humans develop, they start to make certain perceptions of what is good or bad, desirable and avoidable. People start to develop standards for certain aspects of life, and if they feel as though they're lacking in any way, they might choose to manipulate their reality. Manipulators usually have low self-esteem. They'll lie about how late they slept in to try to make others think they're more of a hard worker.

Criminal advantages could be why someone is manipulative as well. Drug addicts might manipulate their family into thinking they need money for rent or other bills, when really they need it for drugs. They might tell a family member that they're sick and the drugs are the only thing that makes them better. A thief will lie to their friends and family about where they're getting their money. They'll manipulate the truth to others around them, sometimes involving them in the crime, just to have control over the situation.

Everyone has their own reasons why they might be manipulating others, but being the victim is never easy. Manipulators will stop at nothing to get what they want, whether it's money, fame, drugs, or power. Sometimes, those closest to us end up being our master manipulators. The entire situation is difficult, especially when there is an imbalance of how much is being taken versus how much is received.

What Happens to the Victim

A victim of a manipulator will often feel codependent on the person that has been influencing them. Those that manipulate often might be abusive towards someone close to them. The victim of a manipulator will have a false sense of power. They see the manipulator as the one in charge, the one who knows best. They've been made to feel like they have no power, so they end up looking to the manipulator for help, validation, and purpose.

They will start to doubt their own thoughts and feelings. The manipulator has repeatedly made them feel as though they don't have any value.

They will convince the victim that they have no worth in order to invalidate their thoughts and feelings. They don't want the victim to have any power because they need to feel like they are in control. The victim sees themselves as worthless, the other person holding all the value. They will start to wonder why their opinions matter at all. They will identify their own thoughts and emotions with that of the manipulator.

Manipulators often have trouble admitting they are in their current situation. If a victim does recognize what's going on, they usually have to be incredibly careful with how they approach the manipulator. They might use scare tactics in order to keep their victims submissive. Manipulators will not be the first ones to come forward about the abuse of power, as that would be admitting their vulnerability. Once it is identified, it can feel helpless to break free.

It's important for those that feel as though they might be manipulated to gain their voice back. It can be scary, but it can certainly be done. The first step is knowing what makes a manipulator and identifying with how they handle their own thoughts and emotions. Not everyone will be able to confront their manipulation, but many friends, relatives, and partners can overcome their imbalance of power.

Profile of a Gas Lighter

A gas lighter is a type of manipulator that makes the victim question their form of reality. They will say things like "you're remembering it wrong," "you're always so hung up on this," or, "you're acting crazy!" Gas lighters will be the first ones to tell someone that they're overreacting. When confronted with the idea that they might be gaslighting, they will usually become angry and defensive, unwilling to at least confront the thought that they might be exhibiting less than perfect behavior.

The term started popping up around 1944 after a movie about a man that tries to convince his wife she's insane became popular. The movie, *Gaslight*, was about a woman, Paula, that married a man, Gregory, and moved to the secluded home of her aunt after her murder. Paula starts to worry when things go missing and strange things start happening in her home, her husband Gregory telling her that she's going insane and imagining it all. One thing included her noticing the gaslight go on at night, her husband claiming she was just imagining it. All along, Gregory had been deceiving her, and was the actual murderer of Paula's aunt. The term caught on and began referring to any situation in which one person makes another feel as though they are insane.

Gas lighters continue this unhealthy behavior in order to gain something from the victim. They might be covering up a lie. A man that's cheating on his girlfriend will tell her she's acting crazy if she questions where he has been. A teenage girl might tell her mother that she's crazy for wondering where she was, even though that girl was at a party she wasn't supposed to be at. A friend might tell the other they're being dramatic if that friend brings up something that emotionally hurt them.

Gas lighters will not admit that they are wrong, and when they are confronted with an opposing view, they'll redirect that suspicions onto the other person. Instead of admitting their own flaws, they'll do their best to turn the attention to their opponent's shortcomings. Gas lighters are dangerous manipulators that should be treated with caution.

Subtle Manipulation

Manipulation isn't always so blatantly obvious. While some victims don't even realize they're being manipulated, there are many manipulators that don't realize what they're doing either. There are some obvious forms of manipulation, but there are also many more subtle versions that not everyone will always notice. This kind can be tricky, and often so insidious that it can be hard to recover.

If the manipulator is in a bad mood, then they might make everyone around them miserable as well. Manipulators might sit in the corner, purposely acting sad in order to gain the attention of others. Someone more active might even go as far as to bring the other people around them down in order to make everyone as miserable as them. They'll take whatever kind of attention they can get, even if that means it's negative.

Manipulators might also exaggerate their illness or injury in order to gain more attention. They might use their illness as an excuse for certain parts of their behavior. While there are plenty of ill people that do have legitimate reasons, when they do certain things, it all depends on if someone else is negatively affected. A manipulator that's ill might act rudely to someone, using their illness as an excuse for their hurtful behavior.

Sometimes, it can be hard to determine if

someone's being manipulative or not. It's not as if a person is going to admit right away that they're being manipulative. Once it is recognized, it can be even harder to figure out how to come up with a solution to get over the problem. There are certain tactics that most manipulators use in order for them to get what they want.

Manipulation Tactics

This section will take you through common manipulation tactics, starting with less serious and moving on towards more harmful forms. Everyone has experienced manipulation differently, but there are certain things that are true in most cases. What makes a manipulator choose to influence people is always going to be different, but how they do it is similar in different cases.

Some manipulators have exhibited behavior like

this all their lives. Their parents might have been the first ones to introduce them to the tactics it takes to manipulate other people. It can be rather devastating to have to revisit childhood, but many people will find that their manipulation behaviors stem from the things they learned as kids. Manipulation might have been a survival tool for some, the only way they knew how to satisfy any of their needs. For others, manipulation might have come from a sibling that felt inferior. Maybe they now look to manipulation as a way to get people to like them, or at least alter their perception.

Other manipulators might only have a few of the common traits found in those that take advantage of others. Even someone that seems like a genuine, caring, and loving person might still be a manipulator to someone in their life. They might even overcompensate for their behavior with others because they're aware of their poor treatment on a certain person in their life.

Manipulation can be tricky to spot, but it's crucial

to do so in order to stop the cycle. What is blatant manipulation to one person might be a way of life for the other. We all have different experiences that account for various aspects of our life, but it's important to always be aware of the way we interact with ourselves and others in order to continually improve our quality of life.

Humor Aimed at Your Weaknesses

Some manipulators will use humor in order to mask their deception. They'll make little jokes here and there that seem harmless but have deep-rooted intentions of manipulation. They'll joke about things they might know that you're sensitive about, or perhaps things to make you feel like less of a person. The manipulator is attempting to make you feel less than them. They're belittling you to make you feel small and to attempt to build themselves up.

These might include subtle jokes like, "It's nice to see that you actually got out of bed today." They are attempting to make a person feel as though they sleep too late on a regular basis. Or a deeper jab like, "Your hair looks nice for once." You'll be blindsided by the compliment, only to then realize that they managed to insult you every other day that they'd seen you. Manipulators will often make these jokes in front of a group of people as well to really diminish your credibility with your friends and family.

They'll then usually make you feel as though it's not fair to get upset over their humor. They'll say things like, "Learn to take a joke," or, "Just laugh at yourself." Manipulators will want to make it feel as though you're in the wrong for being sensitive over the joke. They'll want you to believe that you are the one with the problem and they did nothing wrong.

Manipulators will make other people the butt of the joke in an attempt to approve their self-esteem. They'll attempt to point out someone else's flaw just so they don't have to look at their own. Someone that has insecurities about their weight might make jokes about someone else's, hoping that those around them forget about the state of the manipulator.

There is a grasp at power here. The person being manipulated will feel as though they no longer have any value. They'll be made to see themselves as a joke. Any feelings or sensitivities they have over these jokes will become meaningless to the victim. They'll feel like their own thoughts don't matter, believing everything that the manipulator said about their insecurity.

Surprise and Little Time

A manipulator might use the pressure of time in order to influence other people. They'll make them feel as though they have to rush to have a final decision in a situation that would normally require more time.

Giving a person little time to make a decision puts a lot of pressure on them. They feel stressed and nervous, depending on the aggressor in order to feel a sense of relief. The manipulator then gets what they wanted all along.

Surprise is another manipulation tactic that is often used. A manipulator will attempt to overload their victim with something that's hard to process. They then won't have time for the proper response, so the manipulator wins.

Imagine two people in a relationship, one wanting to buy a new car and the other consistently denying that request. The manipulator might show up with a new car, not giving the other person any time to have a proper reaction. It was such a big purchase that the one who didn't want the car feels as though they now have to give in. What other choice do they have?

By not allowing enough time for a proper reaction, a manipulator is deciding how their victim is going to feel for them. They give them no other choice but to submit to the manipulator.

Lying About and Exaggerating Facts

A manipulator will often exaggerate the truth in order to convince the other person of what might benefit the aggressor. They might say something like, "I could go to the store, but traffic was really bad earlier, so it might be a while," even though they know traffic was at a normal level. They'll take the truth and stretch it as far as they have to in order to convince those around them of the lie, they need to cover themselves. They will say what they have to in order to get the other person off their back.

A manipulator will take any small piece of information and exploit it to the maximum. If their leg hurts after helping a friend move, they'll make sure to bring that pain up as much as possible in order to make their help look like more than it was. They might also say something at one point, completely lying and saying the opposite later. They'll be so detached from reality that they won't be afraid to blatantly lie about the things they may or may not have said.

Manipulators will also straight up lie about the truth. They might say that they were studying all night, when really they were cheating on their girlfriend. They might say that they hadn't done drugs in a month while high. Manipulators will stop at nothing to make someone else believe whatever they have to in order to reach their goals. They aren't afraid of being caught in a lie either, because they'll just lie their way out of that. Some manipulators are so bad that they'll use every tool at their disposal just to cover up one little lie.

Some manipulators are so far into their delusions that they'll end up believing the lie. They won't even react normally when confronted because they'll legitimately believe they did or didn't do what they're being accused of. They are shameless in their lying because they actually end up believing their delusions.

Giving You the Upper Hand

A manipulator will make you feel as though you're in charge. They'll give the illusion that you have the power in the situation. They'll try to tell you what to do but then say things like, "but you're in charge," so that if something does go wrong, the manipulator won't be blamed.

A manipulator might let you speak first, making you believe that you're in control of the situation. You might end up realizing that they only did this in order to hear your weaknesses first and build their argument. They'll give you the chance to state your argument first, but instead of actually listening to your thoughts and feelings, they'll just be meticulously planning their next manipulation.

Manipulators will ask you questions with the impression that they're compassionate. Instead of listening to your answers, they're actually forming their own responses to use against you. They'll trick you into thinking they're listening, but they're actually just breaking apart what you're saying in order to use it against you. They'll listen closely and even take exact phrases of what you said, twisting them and using them against you later.

A manipulator might invite you to their home when discussing something, using this power balance to their advantage. They'll make you believe they're being hospitable even though they are trying to gain the upper hand themselves.

Manipulation as a Positive

Not all manipulation has to be bad. There is certainly a negative connotation surrounding the word manipulation. It is often associated with abusive people that only take advantage of others. That is certainly true in a way, as most abusers use manipulation tactics to get what they want. More often than not, in fact, examples of manipulation turn out to be negative. Not every instance of manipulation has to be negative, however. There are certain ways that manipulation can be used positively.

Think of it like a tool. Manipulation is similar to a hammer. You can either use it to destroy something or create something new. The act of having control is a very powerful position. That power can either be used for good, or it can be used for bad. If you know the password to someone's computer, you can use that to login and look at their information, or you can simply ignore it. If you find a wallet in a bathroom, you can take the cash and toss the wallet, or you can turn it into the front desk. If you know someone's weaknesses, you can use that to exploit them, or you can help improve their life, encouraging them when they feel weak.

Most will use manipulation to their advantage, and this is dangerous behavior. It's important to recognize that not everyone who exhibits manipulative behavior is using it negatively. Some people see manipulation as a survival tactic. They might manipulate others because they legitimately think they know what's best. Many children are manipulative, but not because they're evil. Children are just figuring out how to interact with other people, and the way our actions have power over others is important to discover and dissect.

Positive Social Influence

Social influence is the way in which our society, and the people around us, has developed ideals to influence the individuals in those institutions. Social norms, religion, morality, and ethics all influence how we interact and shape our own personal views. Social influence is derivative from three varieties. The first is compliance, which involves keeping your opinions to yourself, even if they're different from others. The second is identification, which is the influence from someone that is respected and admired. The third is internalization, which is when an idea, behavior, or belief is accepted, and everyone agrees privately as well as publicly.

Social influence can be harmful, but there are also instances in which it can be positive. An example might be a doctor using their persuasion to make their clients believe a certain thing. They'll believe a disease is best treated with a certain medication, so they'll manipulate their patient to take that, with no ulterior motives or attempt at personal gain.

There might also be campaigns directed towards educating users on certain things that need to be changed in society. For example, think of the commercials that are aimed towards getting people to quit smoking. They can be very manipulative in behavior, sometimes exaggerating certain truths and using fear tactics. This manipulation isn't aimed at anything other than trying to benefit both parties.

Not All Manipulators are Evil

If someone is identified as being a manipulator, that doesn't mean that they're automatically evil. Everyone has different reasons why they might be attempting to manipulate those around them. There are always better ways to confront issues than to use manipulation tactics, but sometimes, this is all someone knows. They might not be aware of how to properly express their emotions, so instead they'll use manipulation tactics to try and get what they want.

Think of it like a girl that sees her sister struggling in every aspect of her life. Maybe the sister is failing her classes, addicted to alcohol, and avoiding paying her bills. The girl might use manipulation tactics to try to get her sister to improve her behavior. She's not necessarily evil, she just wants what's best for her sister, and maybe believes tricking her into doing something is going to provide a better result for both of them.

Manipulation is usually a form of avoiding a bigger truth. Maybe humor is used by a wife to joke about her husband's hair, when really, she should just be honest and say that he needs a haircut. The husband might not agree, but at least he won't be made to feel like less than himself by his wife's cruel humor. While not everyone that uses manipulation is necessarily bad, they should still try to confront the bigger issue at hand before using deceptive tactics on their loved ones.

Overcome Manipulation

Once manipulation is identified, the next step is to get through it. Overcoming manipulation can be very challenging. In some cases, a 60 year-old-man might realize just now that his 85 year-old-mother is manipulative. They might never get through their issues, but they should still be confronted. Manipulation takes a part of both the abuser and the victim. It can ruin people's lives, altering the direction they take and affecting the rest of their years. Manipulation can be hard to identify and even harder to overcome.

It can be done, and it should be attempted to get through. In a relationship based around manipulation, there might not be any coming back. Sometimes, people might just have to break up. You might have to get a divorce or stop calling your mom. It takes two people to partake in a manipulative scenario. Not both people will end up identifying it as a manipulative situation, however. In that case, the person that realizes what's actually going on might just have to move on, the manipulator never realizing the damage they caused.

This can be a challenging part of overcoming manipulation. Usually, some instance of codependency formed, making it even harder to break away. There are ways to overcome this, and we will cover that in the next few sections.

Know Your Worth

The first step in overcoming manipulation is for the victim to identify that they still have value. A manipulator likely took everything from their victim. They belittled them, ridiculed them, and made them feel as though what they thought didn't matter. In some situations, they might have even used gaslighting tactics to make their victims feel as though they're insane. It can be hard for a victim to then recognize just how much value they still have once they become aware of the manipulation.

It's important for everyone to know, no matter who is reading this, that you have worth. Everyone has value. No one deserves to be manipulated. No one deserves to feel as though they don't have any purpose, reason, or value. You have the right to be treated justly, and with respect from other people. You are allowed to express your emotions, feelings, wants, and opinions. No one else has the right to tell you how to feel. You set your own boundaries, and no one else gets to decide for you.

If you feel sad about something, that is completely valid. No one gets to decide if what they say hurts you or not. Not everyone might intentionally mean to hurt you, but that doesn't mean you're not allowed to still feel bad. You have the right to feel the way you do, and you have the same right to express those beliefs.

If you feel like you need to protect yourself, you are just in doing so. If you feel like your safety is being threatened, or someone is taking advantage of you, you have the right to remove yourself from that situation without guilt. No one gets to treat you badly, and though that can be hard for many of us to hear, it's the truth.

Manipulators aim to take these thoughts away. They want to deprive their victims of their rights in order to work towards getting what they want. This can't happen anymore. It's up to the manipulator's victims to now recognize their worth and stop the cycle of manipulation.

Don't Be Afraid to Keep Your Distance

Many people that feel as though they're being manipulated end up being too afraid to do anything about it. They have been stripped of their own thoughts and opinions, their own feelings invalidated and instead focus on how other people feel. Those that have been continually manipulated might be afraid to leave those that have hurt them. They've depended on those that abused them for so long they don't know where else to go.

You're allowed to keep your distance. You don't have to feel guilty about protecting yourself. It can be hard to separate yourself from a manipulator, especially in a romantic relationship. You might see the very weaknesses that cause their manipulative behavior. Maybe in a relationship, a boyfriend's dad was an abusive alcoholic, and it greatly hurt him. It also caused his violent manipulative behavior that led him to hitting his girlfriend on a few occasions. It's true that he has his own pain, but that doesn't mean he's allowed to inflict it on others. The girlfriend has every right to leave her boyfriend and find her own peace and protection.

Ask what is really lost by leaving the person that's manipulating you. More often than not, value in a relationship is placed on codependent tendencies. A person is afraid to leave not because they love their manipulator, but because they are afraid to be alone. It can be scary to be on your own, but mostly because manipulators put that idea in their victims in the first place. Manipulators will trick their victims into staying with them because deep down, they know that the victim will be just fine without them.

It's Not Your Job to Change Them

Once manipulation is recognized, the next step is to try to talk to the person about the manipulation. It's time to get down to the root issues of the relationship and figure out what can be done to help both partners get what they need, instead of just the manipulator. There has been an imbalance of power for far too long, and it's time to rebalance.

Unfortunately, not many manipulators are willing to admit their faults and later change their behavior. Instead, they'll do whatever they can to distract others from their faults, placing the blame on their victims instead. When this happens, the victim has to accept that their manipulator isn't going to change, and they must find the strength to leave.

There will likely be a desire to change the other person and help them improve their life as well. Not everyone will always be on the same page of their journey towards self-discovery. It can be hard to accept for some victims, but they have to realize that it's not their job to change their manipulator.

You can only help a person so much, and if they're not willing to change or improve themselves, it's not going to happen. Many people wait around for the other to change in their relationship, hoping their manipulation will get better. If a person isn't aware of their behavior and aren't actively trying to change it, nothing is going to happen in the end.

Confronting the Manipulator

By this point, there should be a comprehensive understanding of what a manipulator is, why they might be manipulative, and what the common tactics of manipulation are. Once this identification has been made, the next step is to move on from the unhealthy cycle that has manifested.

This will usually involve confronting the manipulator. Often, the manipulator might not be aware of what they're doing. There's a good chance that if a conversation is attempted and an actual discussion starts, a person will realize what they have done and might actually try to improve on their manipulative behavior.

Other times, a person might become very defensive, not wanting to admit it to the people that they have hurt. Some people won't be strong enough to recover because they don't want to have to look into themselves and admit their flaws. They've spent so much time internalizing their own self-hate that they aren't capable of confronting the truth. Part of overcoming manipulation is accepting that it's okay to be flawed. Many people have done things that have hurt others, but that doesn't mean all hope is lost.

Sometimes, manipulators are so abusive that they won't be able to come down from their power trip at all. These people should be handled with caution. If a confrontation might lead to physical abuse, it should be avoided, or only done in the presence of others so as to avoid violence. Every manipulator is different, but there are some tactics that can be used to help stop the manipulation in its tracks.

Ask Questions

When manipulation is detected, it's important to start asking questions. Those start with the victim asking themselves questions first. Question whether or not you're being treated with respect. Is what this person asking of you fair? Are they putting you in a position that they know makes you uncomfortable? Is there a big imbalance of power in the relationship?

Once this is done, the victim of the manipulation will be able to easily identify if they are being taken advantage of. They can then form the basis for their confrontation in order to have a healthy and productive conversation with the person that was being manipulative in the first place.

It is also helpful to ask the manipulator questions

when they might be trying to influence others. A victim of manipulation might ask their abuser if their request seems reasonable. Would they ask the same thing of another person? Would they do the same work themselves? Is the person being asked, or are they being demanded? Do they actually have a choice in the matter?

By asking these important questions, a mirror is created, and the manipulator is forced to look at themselves. They have to see what they're doing to their victim, and in a way, they are being confronted with the truth. They might not have even asked these things of themselves, so it might not be until now that they realize how much damage they have been doing.

Take Your Time

The manipulator might use tactics of speed or time pressure to get what they want. This is done in order to distract their victims and not give them a chance to really think everything over.

By taking your time, you allow an opportunity to really make the right decision. You make the manipulator know that you aren't going to be scared into saying yes or no. If you're not sure what to say, always just tell the manipulator that, "you'll think about it." This is not giving them a definitive yes or no. It's letting them know that you're actually going to put time into analyzing the request, deciding if it's something that's actually going to be good for you or not. Many people will be afraid to say this, as they don't want to upset anyone else. You have to know that your feelings take priority, and anyone that is really rushing you for an answer might have manipulation motives.

Many jobs and bosses will use speed tactics to get what they want. They'll offer you a position with a certain salary but tell you that you need to decide quick, so they can let someone else know if they got the job. Anyone that tries to sell something will use time pressure, making the person questioning their purchase know that others might buy it up first. This kind of manipulative tactic works well, but if it's there, it's usually best to just take your time in making a decision.

Practice Saying No

Something that can be incredibly challenging for victims of manipulation is the ability to say no. Manipulators usually make those around them feel as if saying no isn't even an option. They'll make them believe that if they say no, they'll lose something. Manipulators are all about taking from others, so of course, they're skilled at forcing people to say yes as often as possible. They'll use guilt, shame, and embarrassment to force someone to give in. When it comes to overcoming manipulative scenarios, it's crucial to say no when needed.

Saying no can be very powerful. Telling someone that you're not available, what they're asking makes you uncomfortable, or that you just have to say no isn't easy, but it's crucial in overcoming manipulative scenarios. Saying no sets boundaries. It lets others know what you're comfortable with and what you're not. Saying no is sometimes about trusting your gut. Those that have been manipulated for long periods of time no longer trust their gut. They've been made to feel as though what they think and feel is invalid. It's important for them to get back to a place that they can rely on the feelings in their stomach. No one should be put through an uncomfortable scenario because they're too afraid to say no.

If someone is mad that you said no, they probably weren't good for you in the first place. Some people will find that if they start saying no more often, they'll lose a friend, or a certain person will stop talking to them. While it can be scary to be alone, this is actually a good thing. It helps a person realize who is a real friend and who was just there because they knew they could get them to say yes.

Chapter 2 – NLP

Richard Bandler John Grinder developed the idea of NLP in Santa Cruz in 1976. NLP stands for neurolinguistic programming; neuro focusing on neurology, linguistics referencing language, and programming referring to the function of that neural language. These men studied three individual's abilities to change their thoughts and feelings. Many people have adopted their ideas, though criticism still remains around the legitimacy of their study results.

NLP should be thought of not as a process to use on other people, but on yourself. The basic idea of NLP is to change the thoughts and feelings of oneself. Doing this can relieve anxiety, depression, and other mental illnesses. They might feel as though a certain thought or belief holds them back, and by changing one's feelings on this, they can change their life. An example would be a person that decides to make themselves believe they like exercising. Some people have found success in using NLP tactics, though many people have criticized the capabilities of the process as well.

There are certainly some benefits to neurolinguistic programming, but many people use this as a manipulation tactic. The intention of NLP tactics is to be able to look into oneself to figure out what makes them an individual. What forms a person's beliefs can also indicate their quality of life. By changing these beliefs, they can improve a certain aspect of their life. Some manipulators use NLP tactics to convince others to do things that will benefit the manipulator.

In order to understand how someone might be using NLP to manipulate you, it's important to first understand what exactly NLP tactics are. There is some positivity in this way of thinking, so even those that don't find this in their lifestyle in the form of manipulation might still benefit by following this thought process.

How We Receive Information

Our worlds are created based around what we put focus on. What we put our energy into will build the foundations for which we think, feel, express, love, work, and do everything else in our lives that makes us an individual. A person that lives in Beverly Hills has a much different world than someone from the middle of nowhere in Texas. While both are humans born in the United States, they live much different lives, with varying perspectives, beliefs, and morals. You only notice what you tune in on.

Your own world is different than the one around you. For example, someone could go their entire lives not realizing how many car dealerships are on their normal route to work. They might take the same streets to the same place, day after day, week after week, year after year, never realizing they pass three car dealerships. Then the time comes when their car breaks down, and they have to buy a car. Once buying a car becomes that person's goal, they suddenly realize its relevance in the world.

This is often why people will see "signs." Signs are usually our minds just looking for outside validation for something that we want. Perhaps someone is considering whether or not they should have a child. Maybe they see a woman holding a baby on the bus, and then another time they notice a baby commercial. This person considering whether or not to have children might take these as "signs," when really, they signaled their brain once the dilemma started. Their subconscious became alert of all things baby, trying to pick up on signs all around them to help answer whether or not they should have a child.

Some people could go their entire lives without realizing there's something right in front of their face, and then one day, there's a trigger that awakens their newfound alertness.

Your Personality Profile

This is what helps us determine what information we're going to store. What are your interests, what are your hobbies? What are your pet peeves? What makes your skin crawl? What keeps you up at night? What do you hope for the future? These important questions, the ones that make us unique individuals, are what make up our personality profiles.

We all have our own agenda. Whether you're aware or not, you have a reason that you do what you do. If you want to be wealthy, you look for ways that you can make and save money. If you don't want to work but want money, you might find ways to take advantage of other people to get what you want. Everyone has a different motive, agenda, reason.

Goals can be as general as wanting to be rich, or as specific as wanting to be the ultimate pizza eating champion of a small town in Missouri.

Some people are very aware of their goals and actively try to contribute to their goal progression on a daily basis. Others aren't quite sure of their motives and continue to go through life based on basic survival tactics.

Your personality profile determines how you take in information and what you end up doing with that. The main forms of consumption, such as social media, television, and other dark corners of the internet, play into our personality profiles. The thoughts and beliefs our friends and family share with us contribute to our personality profile. Even our physical descriptions, whether we're fit or fat, masculine or feminine, old or young, all contribute to our personality profile as well.

The Animalistic Nature of Our Brain

When deciding to take in the things around us, there are certain questions we start to ask. Is this safe or not? That can be the first instinct for many people, even those that aren't as aware. They might sense danger, whether it's from a shady person or not wanting to live in a specific area of a neighborhood.

Does this have value? This is another question we consider when making decisions. Putting value on certain things differs from person to person, but there is some level of questioning something's worth when presented with making a decision.

Does this help me accomplish something? Is this job, relationship, tool, or other idea meeting some of our needs?

These needs and wants are derivative of our biology. We want money because we want to buy food because if we don't eat, we'll die. This is an obvious one. A subtler natural reaction of our brain is our desire to fit in. When we lived in a world where forming groups was necessary for survival, we developed an urge to prove our worth. A normal "tribe" would have hunters, gatherers, security, and other roles necessary for the survival of everyone. Not everyone was a hunter or a gatherer, but everyone had their worth and they would do what they had to in order to prove their value.

We still have this desire, but it reflects in different ways. We want to prove we have value, so people keep us around, but some people end up mistaking that. A woman might get breast implants to prove that she's beautiful, and she puts value on her beauty. A man might sleep with hundreds of women in order to prove his masculinity.

When we understand our natural biology, that urge that exists in everyone to prove their worth, it can be easier to start to redirect our thoughts.

Our Map of Reality

What everyone around them perceives is completely different. Even a set of twins could have an opposite outlook on life. It's more likely that two people from different geographical or religious backgrounds would have different viewpoints. Still, those that are from seemingly similar places might have completely different perspectives on what reality might look like.

Social influences play a huge part in how a person acts and develops. The background of the people in a community can affect everyone. If most people come from affluent backgrounds, they will all have similar perspectives, forming the viewpoints of those that grow and function in that specific area. If more people are involved in crime in a certain area, it's likely that lifestyle will affect others around. It isn't true for everyone, but location can play a huge role in how a person thinks.

The biological makeup of a person is very important as well. Someone with a family history of anxiety and depression will directly affect their personality and the way they interact with other people. Biological influences beyond just the wiring of our brain play an important part in the mapping of our reality as well. Beyond just mental genetics, hair, skin, and eye color can play into a person's personality, thought processes, and beliefs as well.

Whether nature or nurture plays a more important role is a highly debated topic. It's likely that there is a blend of both that vary from person to person that affect how someone thinks. The family a person was born into, and how they were raised after birth, both greatly affect how a person will act and think throughout their entire lives.

Meaning is Subjective

Since our realities are so different, meaning will become varied as well. Some think the meaning of life is to serve a higher power, such as a god or set of gods. Others think the meaning is to find happiness, while some don't think there's any meaning at all. Our personality profiles, animalistic behaviors, genetic biology, and social upbringing will end up defining our own individual meaning.

Meaning is also subjective because it can be altered at any one time. Someone could go their entire lives believing in God, eventually deciding they're atheist. The opposite could happen too. Some people think they'll never lose their faith, or gain faith, but end up surprised at how quickly they can change their thoughts.

Religion is so tricky because no one was born believing one thing. They might have always felt a certain spirituality deep down, but the major parts of Buddhism, Muslimism, and Christianity were all things that were taught. Meaning is taught to us in a certain aspect, but we also create our own definitions and meanings as well.

The meaning of life might never be clearly defined for every individual, but everyone has their own ideas on what's most important in their life. If they don't, that ends up affecting how they think and act as well. There's power in knowing that you can change your mind at any time, but unfortunately, not everyone will realize this freedom in their life.

NLP practices aim to help everyone realize that they hold the power within themselves to change their lives. They can look inside, figure out what's wrong, and change their perspective on any one thing. Not everyone is going to be able to do this easily, but everyone can at least try.

Since meaning is so subjective, it can be easy to alter what others think. Many people are so lost in what they actually believe that it can be easier to latch onto the ideas of others. This kind of thing is what can become manipulative and harmful. Some who follow NLP practices end up taking advantage of others because they know they can plant different ideas in their brains. They can alter the feelings of others, giving what they're masking as a "solution" to the lost individual's problem. In reality, it's all just something that's going to help the manipulator get closer to their goals.

We Can Change Our Feelings

People can change their feelings when it's convenient. This can be a manipulation tactic used to persuade and control other people. Someone could go their entire lives not caring if their sibling borrowed their clothes. Then, one day, they're mad at their sibling for something else, so they flip out when their sibling borrows their clothing. This is a small example of this tactic, but it's seen often in various relationships.

Many feelings are very hard to overcome, but there are certain people that will take things as far as they can. As we get older and our meaning changes, of course, our feelings will as well.

Not everyone will change the way they think. Some people will go their entire lives with the same feelings, but the truth is, they can be changed at any time. Humans seek comfort, just like many other animals. They don't want to change their thoughts and beliefs because they're afraid of the change that it might ignite. This can lead to very destructive behavior, as unhealthy patterns lead to a stunt in personal growth.

Some people might have an easy time changing their feelings while others find it debilitating to attempt to think in any different way. There are some people that seem as though they're changing their personal beliefs daily. Others will be incredibly stubborn in changing their minds, even if it means their decisions affect the lives of other people that think differently than them.

How People Use This Against You

Once your world is defined, it can be easy to pinpoint all the things that make your world unique. Some people will start to exploit this individuality, trying to connect with you on a personal level. For example, someone might notice that you like henna tattoos, so maybe they get one in an attempt to get closer to you. They end up only doing this because they want something from you. The manipulator is breaking into the person's individual world, disguising themselves as someone they can relate to, when really, they're just trying to distract them to get close.

People will make you rethink your choices based upon your own world. They might make you question, does this fit in with your beliefs? Are you sure you're not going against anything you believe in? These master manipulators will make you question your own morals, and when your beliefs become vulnerable, they'll swoop in and try to take advantage of that.

If someone knows that you're a religious person, they might use religion against you. They'll play on your weaknesses, knowing that as a religious person, breaking your moral code can cause great pain. They can use guilt and other manipulation tactics pertaining to the things that matter to you in order to get what they want.

Mimicking Body Language

Those using NLP tactics will often begin to mimic the body language of another person in order to feel connected to them. If a person is standing with their hand on their hip, the NLP user will do the same thing. If someone is overly confident, puffing their chest with their arms tightly crossed, the NLP user will do this same thing. They'll try to match their body with the other person to make a connection, letting them know they're someone they can trust and depend on.

They might even start talking like them, and they'll certainly give into other ideas as well. If someone is overly enthusiastic, an NLP user might feed on that enthusiasm, exerting a good mood and overall happiness as well. The opposite is true too in terms of personality. If someone seems overly pessimistic, complaining often and sharing negative views, the NLP user will try to match this, giving off the same attitude.

They might even touch the other person in order to gain some sense of connection. This can be very violating, but some people feel so thrown off by this touch that they don't even notice they're being manipulated. This can happen a lot in the workplace and even in school. Maybe a teacher or boss comes up behind a worker and places a hand on their shoulder, their way of exerting their power over the other person. In order to not create an uncomfortable situation, most people just allow the other person to touch them, giving the power to the person that did the touching in the first place.

In order to avoid this, try to do strange things you wouldn't normally do, and see if they begin to do the same thing. Find a funny trick to do with your hand, like maybe tapping the top of your head lightly. Move your eyes around rapidly and tilt your head to the side back and forth. If the person you're talking to begins to do this as well, there's a good chance they might be using NLP tactics.

The same goes for anyone that touches you. If you don't want to be touched, call that person out. Ask them to not touch you nicely, and you'll be surprised to find that they'll let up. The teacher or boss that always seems to put their hand on your shoulder likely won't after the first time you ask them not to because they know it's strange behavior.

Some people actually just adopt the behaviors around them because that's part of their personality. This is a result of codependency, and not always necessarily a manipulation tactic. In order to decipher someone's true intentions, you have to look at what they might gain from the situation. If they don't seem to be taking anything from the other person, it's usually harmless behavior.

Cold Reading

Cold reading is when a person tries to convince you that they know more than they do. Mentalists, mediums, fortune tellers, and psychics will often use this technique to convince you that they are more aware of you and the information pertaining to your life than they actually do. Those that know how to cold read can quickly pick up on your body language and verbal cues to gain a quick understanding of who you are and how you work. These cold readers will use a set of guesses to figure out information, analyzing body language and other responses to figure out whether they are right are not.

For instance, a psychic might start by telling a group of people that they are speaking to someone that has passed with a name that starts with "J." Most people in the audience likely know someone that has died with a "J" name, so they will start to assume the psychic is talking about the person they know. An audience member might speak up by saying, "my uncle Joe just died,' and then the psychic will play off their body language, making small general guesses that the audience member can relate to their life.

The psychic will use verbal cues to tell if they are making the right guesses. If a participant sounds sad, they know they have hit on their emotions and can use this to their advantage. If they seem confused or distant, the psychic knows that they still need to use caution when proceeding with their readings. Anyone who states that they can talk to the dead, see the future, or make predictions and assumptions about yourself is likely highly trained in reading verbal and facial cues in order to produce a convincing cold reading.

Confusing Phrasing

Those using NLP tactics love gibberish. They'll say quick phrases or hide words in bulky sentences in order to sneak in the real meaning of what they're trying to say. This is seen most often in advertisements. Maybe there will be an overload of information. Listen to a commercial in which a medication is being advertised. The entire commercial will be about how great the medication is, the last few seconds a quick reading of the warnings and cautions that come along with taking a certain pill. The same kind of thing can be seen in different interactions with various people. Kids and teens are pretty good at this. They'll ask permission for something, starting first with the reasons why someone would say yes. Then they'll quickly mention all the reasons their parent would say no, like the fact that there won't be parents and it's a co-ed sleepover.

Someone that is using neurolinguistic programming will also be very vague with what they say. They might use quick jargon to try to distract you, or they'll be so general you really aren't sure what their actual intentions are. Think back on different political phrases that were popular. Obama simply used "Change," which could appeal to anyone. Many manipulators will use vague sayings to appease those around them. They'll say, "I'll take care of it," without offering any real explanation as to how they're going to fix the problem presented. Other manipulators might include those that leave out information that could alter perspectives, sharing only general information.

Many psychics are able to have mild success because they're so general with their information. They'll start by asking someone if they've suffered a loss. Well of course, most people have. Even if it's your grandma's old best friend's cousin's dog, everyone knows someone that's died. Certain levels of spirituality are up for debate. There are still those individuals that are able to manipulate others using general information that can be applicable to anyone's perceptions, beliefs, ideas, morals, and world.

Using Your Wants

Those who are skilled in NLP practices know what you want. That's because they have serious wants too! While everyone has their own unique and individual experiences that set them apart from other people, many of us have similar goals. Achieving fame or fortune is a big one.

Happiness is another main contender for shared wants and needs amongst a wide group of people. Manipulators practicing NLP strategies know what people want, so they use those desires to in turn get what they want.

They'll feed off your emotions, making themselves seem sacrificial in the end. Many of us want to feel important, so some seek others they can help.

Those using NLP tactics are much more dangerous than your average manipulator. They actually study how the human brain works, figuring out how to use this strange process to their advantage.

Studying human psychology is important but should only be done for the sake of exploring more about an individual. It shouldn't be used against someone, and it certainly doesn't seem healthy to mimic a person's interactions just to try to get them to buy into someone.

If you feel as though someone might be using NLP tactics, it's trickier than straight up manipulation, but the same practices should be followed to try to dismantle this deception.

Chapter 3 – Subliminal Persuasion

Subliminal persuasion is a term that's mostly found in advertisement. It's often associated with the idea of tricking someone into picking up a message without their awareness. The persuasion is done on a level that those being persuaded can't initially, or easily, pick up on.

It is yet another manipulative tactic that many people use on those around them. Subliminal persuasion isn't as invasive or harmful as other forms of manipulation, but it can still be dangerous. Of all the other forms of manipulation, this might be one of the hardest to detect as well.

The idea of subliminal persuasion is that its influences are below the detectable conscious human level. Those who are being subliminally manipulated won't be able to realize what's going on until it's far too late. In some cases of manipulation, one can recognize while it's happening. For the most part, many people can go years before they realize that they were subliminally persuaded.

The Subconscious Mind

Our subconscious mind works so much harder than our conscious one. It pretty much never shuts off and is constantly making decisions for us before we even realize what's going on. Even while we rest our conscious mind, our subconscious one is putting on various movies for us in the form of dreams. The subconscious has so much information that it has to create these delusions, daydreams, and other forms of dissociation in a way to process all that it knows.

Our brain is pretty much limitless. There might actually be a number to how many things we can know, but we haven't found it quite yet. We've only made assumptions on how far we think our brain can go. Even though we can basically pack information into our brain all day, never feeling like we know too much, most of us will just use what we have already.

Our subconscious is powerful. It consumes about 95% of our brain, yet we don't have complete control over it. Our subconscious mind could be why we develop certain fears or might make up why we have certain addictions. For every time you felt as if you didn't know why you were having a certain thought or emotion, there's a good chance your subconscious brain knew exactly why.

Your subconscious mind has been working this whole time you've been slacking off! Remember that one time you stayed up all night to get a test done? You might not have specific recollection of that night, but your subconscious does. It's what's reminding you to get your work done on time so that you don't have to endure the pain you felt the day after pulling an all-nighter ever again.

The key to most of our conscious issues lie directly in our subconscious. Why might a person think dogs are so scary? They can usually look to their subconscious mind and realize that they internalized something dark in their past to make them fearful of dogs.

We'll never be fully aware of our subconscious or the way it works, but that doesn't mean we shouldn't try. The more we can understand about the innerworkings of our brains, the better we'll be at fixing it in the long run.

Subliminal Advertising

Subliminal advertising uses our subconscious against us. They sneak certain thoughts, feelings, and emotions into the things we consume in order to buy into their products more. Some countries have even banned subliminal advertising, knowing just how dangerous this manipulation tactic can be.

Advertisers know how to get into our heads, literally. They sometimes even pay people to watch their advertisements while their brain function is monitored. This is to get an idea of how our brains work while watching advertisements. They'll track eye movement to see what part of the commercial is being studied. All this information is then used against us to specifically sell something. Advertising has broken into our brains, understanding how to sell us something better than our understanding of capitalism, and what it means to be a consumer.

Think of a chocolate commercial as an example. The advertisement might be nothing more than a picture of a peanut butter cup. You see the logo for a moment, but nothing else that tells you to buy the treat. You still get the idea of the candy bar in your head, forcing you to end up buying one next time you're at the store.

While it is most easily recognizable in advertisement tactics, there are many people that continue to use subliminal persuasion in order to get what they want.

Social Media

Social media has seemingly taken over the lives of many people. Not only do people create social media for themselves, but they make pages for their dogs as well! Social media isn't all bad, but it's agreeably inescapable.

The people that you follow on social media are likely using subliminal persuasion on you without you even realizing it. They can alter what the world sees of their life, using pictures, quotes, videos, and other small glimpses into their lives. We see more than we would see of their life in any other context, so we start to use this as our identifying factors for a specific person. Many people still keep in touch with those on social media that they haven't spoken to in a decade. Their in-person perception has faded and now all that exists is who they know them for as a social media personality.

Social media has allowed us to create our own new worlds. You get to pick and choose what other people see. You only post the good stuff if you want, or you can share the bad stuff too in an attempt to make yourself vulnerable and more relatable.

All many users see is a happy face of a baby, but they don't see that the same baby puked all over its mom and the new white rug once the camera turned off.

This manipulation makes many people feel less than themselves. They feel inadequate after comparing themselves to the people online that are living so happily. Many use this form of subliminal persuasion in order to make themselves feel better.

Altering Perspectives

This type of perspective altering is seen in ways other than just social media. There are plenty of manipulators that only give others little bits of information, using a ton of energy to cover up some big secret that they don't want everyone else to know. Everyone deserves their privacy, and not all secrets are meant to be shared. There are certain things that can really change a person's perspective, and it's not always fair to keep this from other people.

Friends and family might only tell you certain parts of their life that they want you to hear, not anything that's bad. Your sister might tell you on the phone that she's doing amazing, when really, her and her husband have been sleeping in separate beds.

Celebrities are the biggest culprits of subliminal persuasion. They go as far as having teams of makeup artists, hair stylists, wig specialists, and wardrobe coordinators to create a seemingly "effortless" look.

How You're Being Subliminally Persuaded

Whether we're comfortable admitting it or not, most people are being subliminally persuaded in one way or another. Many forms of passive aggression can also be forms of subliminal persuasion. Maybe a person's mother makes a comment about how they saw someone at the store they hadn't in a while, making a comment about their weight gain.

This could also be a subliminal message about how the mother feels about her daughter's weight. The subliminal persuasion, then, is that the daughter's perception is now altered. She might feel as though she does not meet her mother's standards of beauty and will alter her life as a result of this mild manipulation.

This is the trickiest of all the persuasion tactics discussed in the book so far.

Those that are doing the subliminal persuasion are usually so lost in their delusions that they'll never recover. They won't be the first to admit that they might carry around some manipulation tactics.

Asking for More

One method that a subliminal persuader uses is to ask for more than they actually need. Perhaps someone needs $5,000, but they know that's a big amount to ask for. So, they'll actually end up asking for $12,000, knowing that's a massive amount of money for someone to borrow. The person they asked might feel bad that they need so much money, and instead offer half in the amount of $6,000 still wanting to help even though they can't give the full amount.

The person that gives in are then under the impression that they have to give at least something. They feel bad for not having enough to give for the original offer. Really, the master manipulator knew all along that they really only needed $5,000.

The person that was subliminally persuaded might end up feeling guilty because they couldn't give more. Even though that person already asked for something once, they can come back because the person that was manipulated still didn't feel like they had given enough.

Doing Favors

Someone that might subliminally persuade another person might first ask for a favor. In some manipulation cases, a person might blatantly tell another what to do, or at least manipulate them in an attempt to get what they want. A subliminal persuader might just ask for the favor, giving the illusion that they are in need of some sort of help.

The person being manipulated feels like they should help out, as they might have a need to care for others. They are also giving the illusion that they are worth doing the favor for.

Those that were subliminally persuaded then might feel as though they're special because they had the privilege of helping another person. They feel good about themselves, like they had value and were helpful to someone. Really, the manipulator just used that need to care to their advantage, getting what they wanted from the person that was manipulated.

This method is seen most amongst bosses. They'll appoint a member of their team to a special position, making them feel like a superior employee. In reality, it was a task anyone could do, and the boss just didn't want to do it themselves.

If you think you might be being subliminally persuaded, it might be a good idea to ask if the person that asked for the favor can do it themselves.

Why might they be asking you? What personal gain do they have when you specifically do the task?

Being Flattered

Flattery is great, but many people use it as a manipulation tactic. They think if they can build someone up and really make them feel good about themselves, then they'll be able to get anything they want out of them.

Children are great at flattery and learn at an early age how to trick people into doing what they want. They understand using charm can lead to happiness in other people, which will lead to them doing things for the manipulator. Most children become aware of this behavior, but many adults continue to practice this subliminal persuasion. A young woman might flatter an older man that isn't all that attractive, but maybe he has money.

This is common in abusive partners as well. They might feel as though they can build up their significant other as much as they want, only to then tear them down at a later time.

Tactically Choosing When to Ask

Those that are being subliminally persuasive will be very calculated about when to ask for something. They'll put effort into deciding when the right time to ask for a favor might be.

They'll choose a time when you might be tired, or maybe even in a really good mood. They'll wait until just the right time to ask for something in order to ensure the person that they are asking will absolutely say yes.

Someone that's subliminally persuading you will also try to only ask in public settings, thinking that they're giving you the upper hand. They'll take away the opportunity for an uncomfortable confrontation. They also might ask in front of friends and family, making the person that's being subliminally persuaded feel as though they're having an opportunity to show off how generous they are.

Conclusion

Anyone has the potential to be a manipulator, just like anyone might find themselves to be a victim of manipulation tactics. There's no set of rules that it takes to become a manipulator, and even the strongest of people might find themselves under the influence of other people's ideas. It usually starts in childhood, though there are other reasons it might develop later in life. Not all manipulators are bad, and sometimes it developed as a survival tactic.

These behaviors can be incredibly dangerous and can ruin people's lives. Some forms of manipulation can be good, like a lawyer advising their clients to accept certain plea bargains. Other forms can be very dangerous, like a holistic doctor denying a patient the right medical care even if they require it for survival.

Not everyone that is a manipulator will be ready to accept that fact. People who exhibit gaslighting tendencies might be resilient to the acceptance that they can be manipulative.

It can be a challenging truth to face, but manipulation has to be recognized in order for more growth to take place. Some people might display aggression when confronted with the idea that they're manipulators. Others might understand that they've been taking advantage of others completely and express a desire to change their behavior.

This book could be read over and over again, but nothing will change unless there is action taken now. It's up to the reader to recognize these behaviors and use their strength to work through their issues. It's not going to be easy for everyone, but it takes time and practice and should be treated with patience throughout the process.

Not every time manipulation is recognized is the time to confront the issue. Sometimes, you will have to sit with the discomfort and just recognize that the other person is trying to take advantage of you. Unless your immediate safety is threatened, don't bring up the manipulation if it's not the right time. If a manipulator is confronted in the wrong setting, it can end up making them internalize their feelings, pushing the reality further down so that they don't have to admit that they're wrong.

A person that admits they have been manipulated can become rather vulnerable. It's important to remember individual worth and value in a process that can sometimes feel so draining. A person that has been manipulated is not weak, dumb, or ignorant. Manipulators are skilled in using other people, and it's not the victim's fault they were taken advantage of.

It might be a challenging process, but it's necessary in order to achieve a higher quality of life. Everyone deserves to have their own voice, and no one should have to experience unfair manipulation.

Thank you!

Before you go, I just wanted to say thank you for purchasing my book.

You could have picked from dozens of other books on the same topic but you took a chance and chose this one.

So, a HUGE thanks to you for getting this book and for reading all the way to the end.

Now I wanted to ask you for a small favor. **Could you please consider posting a review on the platform? Reviews are one of the easiest ways to support the work of independent authors.**

This feedback will help me continue to write the type of books that will help you get the results you want. So if you enjoyed it, please let me know! (-:

www.ingramcontent.com/pod-product-compliance
Lightning Source LLC
Chambersburg PA
CBHW052102110526
44591CB00013B/2319